THE BIG PICTURE OF THE BIBLE

Kenneth V. ....g

DEWARD
PUBLISHING COMPANY

The Big Picture of the Bible
© 2008 by DeWard Publishing Company, Ltd.
P.O. Box 6259, Chillicothe, Ohio 45601
www.dewardpublishing.com

ISBN: 978-0-9798893-2-5

Printed in the United States of America.

Third printing.

Original artwork by Ken Craig. Artwork redrawn and modified for print by Jeff Angelo and Eric Wallace.

DEDICATION AND ACKNOWLEDGMENTS

To Steve Bobbitt—

A near lifelong friend, spiritual mentor, and fellow laborer who showed me by the example of his life that it is possible to give an answer for the hope that is in us with gentleness and reverence.

I also wish to thank a few people who have been particularly encouraging and supportive to me in the production of this book: Dan DeGarmo who has shown me an example of true passion for the lost and "pressured" me to produce it; Steve Wilsher and Ron Roark who continually push me and travel with me to the ends of the world sharing this message; Clark and David Maxson who share their enthusiasm and results in using and propagating this message; Rob van de Weghe, my Dutch friend and brother, whose prodigious work in evidences *(Prepared to Answer)* has strengthened my faith; my church family at Helena that has been very gracious in their support of my gospel efforts; proofreaders Ben Davis, Pam Dial, and Carolyn Maxson; so many of my Christian friends who have acted as "iron sharpening iron"— particularly Beau Christy, Dale Smelser, Bryan Moody, L.A. Mott, Paula and Steve Heltsley, Charlie Nowlin, and Gary Henry—as I pieced this together; and all my immediate family who have allowed me to prioritize my life around the sharing of the gospel and have encouraged my efforts in every way possible.

To God be the glory.

FOREWORD

I first met the author on February 5, 2005 at a seminar in Ocala, Florida. Throughout that morning I sat in my padded pew listening to several presentations regarding various topics all relating to the methodology of Christian evangelism in the 21st century. Make no mistake about it; my attitude was arrogant and indifferent. I grew up at the feet of some prominent theologians and well-spoken preachers. I thought I had heard it all. Then I heard Ken Craig share a presentation entitled "The Big Picture of the Bible"—the same message that you will hear if you give this book just a few minutes of your time.

Upon hearing this message and confidently embracing it as truth, I have passionately shared it with anyone who would give me the time. The response has been nothing but extraordinary. The following account sums it all up quite well. I was speaking in Brownsburg, Indiana earlier this year and following two sessions in which I presented the very same material in this book a middle-aged man walked up to me with tears streaming down his face and simply said, "I finally get it."

Be not alarmed. This book and the message contained on the following pages are in no way some new, unexplored revelation. Countless books have been written about the Bible; this book, however, is unlike any. It is different because it is comprehensive in scope, yet simple to understand. It is unique in that it is undeniably true. It is my hope that the message you will find here will change your life as it did mine on that February afternoon.

Daniel DeGarmo
Chillicothe, Ohio

PREFACE

Why did God create man? Why is the Bible so misunderstood? Why are there so many different churches? What is the Bible really all about? When confronted by one of these or similar questions we are often left groping for answers. This little book is my attempt to provide answers to these and similar questions.

As a college freshman I took a class taught by Ferrell Jenkins on The Scheme of Redemption. For the first time I saw the elegance and unity of the Bible as the events of history unfolded to accomplish God's purposes. With this as a foundation, I began to further focus on the unity found in the spiritual purposes that underlay the historical events. The connections became even more profound. This resulted in a set of lectures called "Seeing the Big Picture of the Bible." This little book attempts to faithfully track these lectures.

This book is neither an apologetic nor a systematic theology, although one friend wryly suggested that it should be titled *Systematic Theology for Dummies*. Rather it is an attempt to present an overwhelming positive case for the unity of the Bible as evidenced by its overall theme.

It is not written for scholars or novices but I hope that it will prove readable and useful to both. Section 1 is the essential message of the book which attempts to describe the overall theme of the Bible. Section 2 presents four testimonies that validate the response of faith to those that have come to belief.

It is my hope and purpose that we will see the Bible as true. While it is a supernatural book, it is not a superstitious book. It is a book of themed purpose, not a bunch of proof texts to be strung together to try to prove anything one desires. Our highest purpose in life is to understand what kind of people our Creator desires us to be and live accordingly regardless of pain or promise.

To God be the glory.

Ken Craig
October, 2009

Christianity claims to give an account of facts—to tell you what the real universe is like. Its account of the universe may be true, or it may not, and once the question is before you, then your natural inquisitiveness must make you want to know the answer. If Christianity is untrue, then no honest man will want to believe it, however helpful it might be; if it is true, every honest man will want to believe it, even if it gives him no help at all.

C.S. Lewis, *God in the Dock*

SECTION ONE

THE BIG PICTURE

And these are but the outer fringe of his works;
how faint the whisper we hear of him!
Who then can understand the thunder of his power?

Job 26.14

1

THE INCREDIBLE BOOK

The Bible is one of the most widely read books in history. It is also one of the most misunderstood. Much of the confusion results from a failure to grasp the overall message or central theme of the Bible. It is a "forest for the trees" problem. Often so much time is spent in the "trees" of different Bible doctrines that we miss the "forest" or big picture. Sometimes we need to step back to see this big picture. Grasping the overall theme of the Bible provides direction for deeper study as well as unity in the understanding and application of its teachings.

Consider a few amazing facts about the Bible:
- It is not just one book, but a collection of sixty-six books of law, poetry, history, narrative, and prophecy (39 Old Testament, 27 New Testament).
- It was authored by more than 40 men with varying degrees of education, different nationalities, and diverse cultures from three continents (Africa, Europe, and Asia).
- It was written in three languages—Hebrew, Aramaic, and Greek.
- It was produced over a period of about 1,500 years.

There are many strong evidences for the inspiration of the Bible that one could consider in the fields of archeology, prophecy, or even science. One of the most intriguing and convincing evidences of the Bible is the internal evidence of the unified message it contains: God's amazing plan to redeem His fallen creatures. Each book reflects a unity of facts, teaching, and purpose supporting this theme. All history unfolded to accomplish God's purpose, and each book of the Bible is a single thread woven into this incredible tapestry. Ordinary men could never have created this book—time, history, and human nature would have prevented its existence and unity unless it was supernaturally directed by God. Its documents have been more critically examined and investigated than any others. The statements of these 40 different authors are reliable and trustworthy.

If we fail to understand the theme of the Bible, it will not matter what we choose to believe or practice in religion. God's plan of redemption, anchored in the writings of the Old Testament, was fulfilled in the New Testament. Here it is called the "gospel," literally meaning "good news." If it is our desire to understand the big picture of the Bible, we must consider and comprehend the importance of this gospel message.

2

THERE IS ONLY ONE GOSPEL

As Jesus prepared to leave earth He gave final verbal instructions to His followers. His last instructions must have been of critical importance to Him—nothing trivial here. These words are His parting command, known today as "the Great Commission." He instructed His followers to *"go into all the world and preach the gospel to every creature"* (Mark 16.15). In His final words on earth, Jesus commanded His followers to go and tell His story—the gospel.

God's Power to Save

Jesus' instruction certainly elevated the importance of the gospel, and Romans 1.16 tells us why: *"For I am not ashamed of **the gospel** for **it** is the **power of God** to salvation."* God could have chosen, as some religions today profess, that people are to be converted at the point of a sword. God could have chosen to take over people's minds and save them against their will. Romans 1.16 tells us that the gospel is the means God uses to save people. It is a message to be communicated to people that can save them—a message from God that stands between man and salvation. As such, the gospel is objective truth.

Second Thessalonians 1.7–8 stresses the importance of the gospel in a different and more serious way: *"When the Lord Jesus will be revealed from heaven with His mighty angels in flaming fire, dealing out retribution to those who do not know God and to those **who do not obey the gospel** of our Lord Jesus."* Our response to the gospel requires obedience.

Because the gospel is so important, a special warning is given to the Christians in the churches of Galatia who were beginning to change the gospel message.

Beware of False Gospels

Paul was amazed that Christians in Galatia were already following *"a different gospel."* The Galatians were preaching a way to be saved different from what they were originally taught! Paul strongly insisted that there is only one gospel (and that they must know it!) by declaring that even should he (an apostle) *"or an angel from heaven teach a different gospel,"* he would be condemned (Gal 1.6–9). The fact that the Galatians were Christians, sincere in their beliefs, and even well-intentioned would not protect them from the promised condemnation if they changed the gospel message.

What Christians were so specifically warned about in Galatians 1 has happened! Consider the following important, politically incorrect observations:

- Different gospels (what people are told about *how to be saved)* exist today. This is the reason there are so many churches today; each church is based on a different gospel, a different way of offering and receiving salvation. Numerous different churches professing to follow Christ are not evidence of an incomprehensible Bible or a failed Christianity. It is evidence that we have failed Christianity!
- Good, sincere people, believers, or churches, can teach *or* follow a different gospel (just like the churches and Christians throughout Galatia).
- Different gospels may be taught by those with considerable knowledge, education, and influence (even apostles or angels!). Just being religious, even sincerely devout, provides no assurance of faithfulness. As Jesus Himself taught: *"Not everyone who says to me, 'Lord, Lord,' will enter the kingdom of heaven, but **only he who does the will of my Father** who is in heaven"* (Matt 7.21–23; see Luke 6.46).
- Each individual is responsible to discern between the one gospel and false gospels by truly recognizing and accepting the one true gospel. I understand that U.S. Treasury agents are trained to spot counterfeit money through intense training and study of genuine money. They become so familiar with the content, smell, look, and feel of genuine money that they can spot a counterfeit immediately. Likewise, Christians are expected to be able to avoid false gospels by knowing the genuine gospel.
- The gospel belongs to God; therefore, no one is to tamper with it—at all!

What would Paul have to say to those today who openly proclaim that nothing matters in our faith as long as we all believe in Jesus? Don't let the fact escape you that the Galatians were definitely believers and followers of Jesus. Knowing and responding to this *one gospel* is *critical* to believers because our salvation depends upon it! Likewise, believing, teaching, or following a false gospel will cause us to be condemned, no matter how educated, famous, religious, or sincere we are—or what church we attend!

So how can we be sure of the one gospel?

Where might we start to find out?

A Progressive Revelation

The Bible is a progressive revelation from God. He revealed Himself bit by bit and stage by stage, each new stage building on those that had preceded it. If you skip the first half of any good book, you will have a hard time understanding the characters, the plot, and the ending. The New Testament is only completely understood when it is seen as being built upon the foundation of the events, characters, laws, prophecies, covenants, and promises of the Old Testament. It shouldn't surprise us then that the New Testament gives us pointers that indicate the important role of the Old Testament. Galatians 3.24 says, *"The old law was given to us as a **teacher** to **bring us to Christ** so that we may be **justified by faith"** (see also Rom 15.4; 1 Cor 10.11; 2 Tim 3.15). The New Testament points us to the Old Testament. In this manner all of Old Testament history was a teaching or training period to prepare mankind for the arrival of Jesus Christ and His role in the plan of redemption. Consequently, a proper grasp of the Old Testament has a very important purpose in understanding the overall theme of the Bible. It was a teaching or learning period for all of mankind.

Some of the things we need to learn from that Old Testament period include the creation of the universe, mankind, and early earth history. But what is in the Old Testament that will *lead us to Christ?*

3

THE ETERNAL PLAN

The Bible begins with the God who was pre-existent before the creation of our physical universe.

We are told in the Bible that God had this plan of redemption before He ever created mankind (Eph 3.11; 1.4). Why would this be so? It has to do with "free will." Free will simply means the ability to choose one's own moral actions without any interference or compulsion. It makes logical sense that if God were going to create a free moral agent—a being that could choose to do right or wrong from its own volition—He would have prepared a plan in advance as to how He would react or handle the result of mankind's choices. This plan of redemption is God's planned reaction to the free moral choice of mankind to sin (break God's laws).

So why did God create man to start with, or even bother with the creation of a physical universe? We cannot get inside the mind of God, so we are restricted to what He has revealed about Himself to His creation (Job 26.14). What God has revealed is that He has purposed to have spirit beings in heaven that choose to love and worship Him out of their own choice. Before God created our physical universe, He had created spirit beings (called angels) in another dimension (called heaven) that had chosen (as free moral agents) at some point to sin against God. He subsequently cast them out of heaven (2 Pet 2.4: *"God did not spare angels when they sinned, but cast them into hell and committed them to pits of darkness, reserved for judgment"*). It was after this, that He created the dimension in which we live (a physical universe) and spirit beings (us), and placed us inside physical containers (our bodies). Just as many computers are labeled with the famous "Intel Inside," each of us should be labeled "Spirit Inside!" It is this spirit, created in the image of God, that separates and distinguishes mankind from the animal world (Gen 1.27: *"God created man in His own image, in the image of God He created him; male and female He created them"*). As spirits, we are placed in these temporary physical containers in order to train our bodies (spiritual and physical) to love, serve, and worship Him for His glory.

Unlike the angels, we have been created as embodied spirits. Our mortal bodies restrict our free moral actions to this dimension, the physical realm. God desires to see if we will choose to love Him, to worship and serve Him, while we experience the trials, tragedies, temptations, and blessings of this life on earth (Deut 8.2; 13.3: *"The Lord your God is testing you to find out if you love the LORD your God with all your heart and with all your soul"*). When our mortal bodies eventually die—the inevitable fate of all humans—our eternal spirits will return to God and await His final judgment, which will determine our eternal fate (Ecc 12.7: *"Then the dust will return to the earth as it was, and the spirit will return to God who gave it"*; Rev 20.13: *"And the dead were judged... according to their deeds"*). We will either join God in our resurrected spiritual bodies (1 Cor 15.43–58) in His dimension (heaven) or will be cast away from His presence (hell). It all depends on whether we live the kind of lives that demonstrates our willingness to recognize Him as our Creator and love and serve Him while here on earth (1 Pet 1.17: *"If you address as Father the One who impartially judges according to each one's work, conduct yourselves in reverent fear during the time of your stay on earth"*). To God, our physical death is not the end of the matter. To have our spiritual bodies cast away from his presence in eternity is of far greater significance than anything that happens to our mortal bodies in this physical realm.

We also see that God uses the analogy of a parent to describe our relationship with Him: He is our Father, and we are His children (1 John 3.1: *"How great is the love the Father has lavished on us, that we should be called children of God! And that is what we are! The reason the world does not know us is that it did not know him"*). What do parents desire?—that their children demonstrate their love to them because they actually want to (out of their own choice)—not out of compulsion (because they are made to). God has made us in His image and this is effectively demonstrated in the love of a parent to a child. It is God's will and desire to have a loving *spirit*-ual relationship with every spirit being that He has created. This relationship must be defined in accordance with His character and nature.

Two Gods?

Some people have drawn the mistaken conclusion that there must be two Gods in the Bible. There is the God of the New Testament that is all love, joy, forgiveness, peace, and happiness, while the God of the Old Testament is an angry God of justice, punishment and wrath.

Clearly we see that God does behave differently towards His creation in the Old Testament than He does in the New Testament. But is He really a different God? No. Consider a parent that lovingly disciplines a small child so that he will learn the things needed to be a productive adult. When my children were little, I, as their father, disciplined them as often as I thought they needed it. They rarely enjoyed it, and, on occasion, would remark, "Daddy, you are mean." At that point in their lives I might have resembled that God of the Old Testament that appeared harsh toward His creation. But now that my children are grown up they have a completely different attitude toward "mean dad." We have a great relationship with our grown-up children on a completely different level than that of the growing-up training period. That is what the New Testament is trying to tell us about the Old Testament period. As pointed out earlier, the Old Testament was a teaching and training period to prepare us for Christ. That included many disciplinary actions toward people and nations that often appear unnecessarily strident or harsh by later standards and behavior. God behaves differently toward His creation in the New Testament, as well as today, on the basis of spiritual maturity learned from the training of the Old Testament period. The God of the Old Testament and New Testament is the same God. *"I the Lord do not change"* (Mal 3.6).

4

GOD IS HOLY

All Biblical understanding must begin and end with a knowledge (as much as possible) of God. The character or nature of God is defined by the characteristic of holiness—the pure absence of any evil—*"You are not a God who takes pleasure in evil; with you the wicked cannot dwell"* (Psa 5.4). John says, *"God is light; in Him there is no darkness at all"* (1 John 1.5). John is telling us that God is completely free from any moral evil: He is the essence of moral purity and goodness. The holiness of God is the very foundation for His plan of redemption.

It is God's **holiness** that perfects His attributes of omnipotence (infinite power), omniscience (perfect knowledge), and omnipresence (present everywhere). Imagine that I, Ken Craig, had the attributes of omnipotence, omniscience, and omnipresence. Would you love me? Or worship me? Not necessarily. What if I were evil—a Hitler or a Darth Vader? It is precisely God's nature of holiness that makes all of His attributes perfectly good. It is His holiness that makes Him worthy of our praise, love, and devotion. I observe His holiness in His interaction with His creation. Consequently, it creates within me a love and reverence for God and a desire to serve Him, and to be forever with Him as my spiritual Father in heaven.

A God of Justice and Love

"For the word of the LORD is right and true. …He loves righteousness and justice; The earth is full of his unfailing love" (Psa 33.4–5). We also discover that God's holiness is demonstrated to us in one of two aspects, His justice and His love. Again: *"Righteousness and justice are the foundation of Your throne; Love and faithfulness go before You"* (Psa 89.14). All of our dealings with God are governed by these two aspects of God's holiness.

God's **justice** means that God will never treat mankind unfairly. We can trust His promises and we can trust His judgments and pronouncements (Deut 32.4; Job 8.3). We can count on the fact that He will do what He says (Isa 46.8–11). Likewise, if God pronounces a penalty or judgment, not only will it be fair and in the best interests of mankind, but we can be sure that He will follow through on His pronouncement.

A complementary facet of God's holiness and justice is His **love** for His creation. While His justice is fair and sure, it is always administered in the context of His love. He loves us as a father loves his children. He always seeks to accomplish in us what is needed to have a loving relationship with Him.

God repeatedly states that we are to be holy because He is holy. *"Thus you are to be holy to Me, for I the LORD am holy; and I have set you apart from the peoples to be Mine"* (Lev 20.26). As observed earlier, God created us as spiritual beings and wants to have a spiritual relationship with His creation. If we are holy we can then, and only then, have the spiritual union that a holy God desires.

This forms the basis for the plan of redemption, God's incredible plan of justice and mercy first demonstrated in the Old Testament. So, why was a plan to redeem mankind needed in the first place?

The Problem of Sin

Breaking God's will, to any degree, is called sin (1 John 3.4). Sin is bad. Nothing defines God's character and His relationship to man as much as His absolute abhorrence of sin. God is God. God is Holy. God is King. Any breaking of His law results in His absolute revulsion to those who reject His will. Sin makes us **un**holy.

5

SIN SEPARATES US FROM GOD

Sin has dire consequences for God's creation. Sin involves us in three deaths that influence our relationship with God and His universe:

Spiritual Death

Because God is holy, any sin—regardless of its motivation, magnitude, or consequences—must result in separation from a holy God. *"Your iniquities have **separated you from your God;** and **your sins have hidden His face from you"** (Isa 59.2; see Hab 1.13). Because He is holy, God must turn His face away when we sin. This separation from God, the essence of spiritual life, is so dreadful it is referred to in the worst possible term, spiritual death (Eph 2.5: *"Even when we were dead through our trespasses, made us alive together with Christ—by grace you have been saved."* See also Col 2.13; Rom 6.23; 1 Tim 5.6). When our *spirit*ual relationship with God is severed, it is as if the spirit inside our "container" has died.

Mortal Death

Spiritual death is not the only result of sin. We all experience consequences of the first sin of humanity. Before sin, man existed in a perfect state of spiritual fellowship with God. As a result of Adam and Eve's first sin in the Garden of Eden (referred to as "the fall") we will all die a mortal death (Gen 3.19). Our "containers" will not live forever. Mortal death will befall us all and is a reminder of the seriousness of sin. Other consequences of the first sin were pronounced as well. Man has to work in difficulty and women will

have pain in childbirth. The earth is no longer a perfect place but now produces natural disasters which affect all creation (see Gen 3.14–24). All of this occurred because of the first sin.

While spiritual and mortal death are consequences suffered by each individual, nothing has been done that would deal with sin, that is, remove sin or restore man's spiritual relationship with God.

6

GOD'S JUSTICE DEMANDS LIFE AS PAYMENT

Judicial Death

There are prices to be paid when we break the laws of any country. For example, when we are caught speeding, we may be required to pay a fine as restitution. If we murder someone, we may be required to spend life in prison or may even be executed. These are penalties executed by a judicial system; they are the judicial price for the breaking of a law. Likewise, there is a judicial price that God requires as His legislative penalty for the breaking of His laws (sin). The price God requires for sin is as serious as its consequences.

The first command of God issued in the Garden of Eden clearly elaborated the judicial price for sin, *"From the tree of the knowledge of good and evil you shall not eat, for **in the day that you eat from it you will surely die**"* (Gen 2.16–17). Put in the plainest of words, God pronounces the payment of death as the price for sin. This is the judicial price for breaking God's law. Life is the price! God pronounced death as the price for sin and His justice must be served. Adam and Eve surely suffered the consequences of sin—they died spiritually the instant they sinned, and they were destined to eventually die a natural, mortal death many years later (see Gen 5.1–5), but that did nothing to remove their sin, or pay the price for their sin—death. The New Testament clearly states the fundamental principle that *"without the shedding of blood there is no forgiveness of sins"* (Heb 9.22).

God presented Adam and Eve with the choice to sin or not sin. It was a choice they had control over. When tempted by Satan, they succumbed. Genesis 3.6 describes it this way, *"When the woman saw that the tree was good for food, and that it was a delight to the eyes, and that the tree was desirable to make one wise, she took from its fruit and ate; and she gave also to her husband with her, and he ate."* We all sin in this way at some point. James described it this way: *"But each one is tempted when he is carried away and enticed by his own lust. Then when lust has conceived, it gives birth to sin; and when sin is accomplished, it brings forth death"* (Jas 1.14–15).

God demonstrated repeatedly throughout the Old Testament the penalty for sin—the death of the sinner (Ezek 18.20: *"The person who sins will die").* Other examples include the Genesis flood and the destruction of Sodom and Gomorrah as described in 2 Peter 2.4–11. Death was a result of their ungodliness.

God's mercy is already demonstrated, to some extent, in that we are not all immediately struck dead (what we deserve) the instant we sin. God takes no pleasure in the death of sinners; He does not have a blood lust, nor is His justice administered capriciously (Ezek 33.11: *"I take no pleasure in the death of the wicked, but rather that the wicked turn from his way and live").*

In summary, because of sin, the Old Testament introduces us to the language of death: 1. Spiritual death – the separation from God of our spirits due to our sin, 2. Mortal death – the death of our bodies as a result of the first sin of Adam and Eve, and 3. Judicial death – the death that is required to pay the price for or atone for our sin.

All Have Sinned

We are all pronounced guilty because we each have sinned. Looking over the scope of history, the New Testament writers reflected this chilling and disturbing characteristic of man by observing that *"all have sinned and fall short of the glory of God"* (Rom 3.23).

We are in a very desperate situation: we have broken the laws of the God of the universe. This has separated us from a holy God, and death is required for payment by a just God. If we die our natural, mortal death in this condition we will be eternally separated from God—another consequence of sin. If I could somehow give my life to pay this price I would receive no benefit as my life has ceased! No one else is qualified to pay this price for me as they are liable for their own sins. What a wretched situation. Can I be delivered from this death sentence?

7

God's Love Provides Mercy

Grace and Mercy

Fortunately, God loves His creation and has decided to help us with this price for sin, even though it was undeserved—this is called *grace* (God gives us what we don't deserve—life). This is also described as *mercy* (God doesn't give us what we do deserve—death). How was His mercy shown in the Old Testament? By blood. The Bible could be said to drip blood if you squeezed it. The Bible is bloody due to the problem and price for sin. God, in His love and His mercy, allowed the price of life to be paid through an innocent representative. This was the purpose of animal sacrifice instituted in the Old Testament. God showed His mercy by allowing the innocent animal to pay the price of death owed by the sinner. We deserved God's justice (death) but we received God's mercy (life) instead. God showed His mercy by allowing an innocent animal to pay the judicial price of death owed by the sinner.

Animal Sacrifice

This provision (or atonement) for the judicial price of sin to be paid by an animal is described in detail in Leviticus 17.11: *"For the life of the flesh is in the blood, and I have given it to you on the altar to make atonement for your souls; for it is the blood by reason of the life that makes atonement."* The life of the animal atones for (pays the price for) or cleanses the sins of the sinner. In this manner the sinner "died" representatively or through the

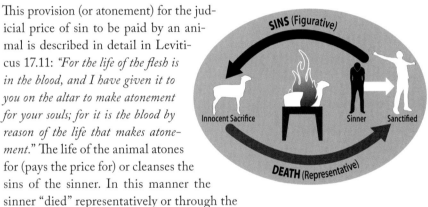

animal as a substitute. What was the result? The removal of sin. In Leviticus 16.30 this result is described as taking place on the Day of Atonement (the yearly sacrifice of animals): *"For it is on this day that atonement shall be made for you to cleanse you; you will be clean from all your sins before the LORD."* This demonstrates the concept of sanctification. To sanctify something is to make it holy and clean before the Lord. Thus by having one's sins removed by animal sacrifice the sinner was made holy before God and the spiritual relationship could be restored (reconciliation).

Notice some basic facts about animal sacrifice:

- The animal was innocent of sin—it was amoral, it couldn't sin. If an animal could have sinned it would have been liable for its own sin! Sinlessness was required for it to provide a representative death.
- The animal had to be physically perfect, spotless, unblemished (see Lev 22.21–27).
- In a single act (animal sacrifice) God demonstrated both His justice (the price of life was paid for sin) and His mercy (the sinner was allowed to live).
- On the basis of the death of the animal the sins of the sinner were removed

and he was made holy (sanctified) and as a result the relationship with a holy God was restored (reconciliation).

Consider this: after Adam and Eve committed the first sin in Genesis 3.1–8 their *"eyes were opened."* They were now aware of their sin, realized they were naked, made clothes from fig leaves, and then they hid from God. They knew they had broken His law and what the penalty was—death! Then in Genesis 3.21 we read a curious statement: *"The LORD God made garments of skin for Adam and his wife and clothed them."* Animal skins come from dead animals; animals died and Adam and Eve continued to live! Although this account was not written to explain the plan of redemption, it is consistent with taking life to pay for sin through the representative death of the animal(s). The foundational elements of the plan of redemption are present on the occasion of the first sin in the Garden of Eden. From this point forward, without any further explanation, animal sacrifice is a common occurrence in the lives of the Old Testament believers.

Sacrifices and related elements are found in practically every culture on the globe. Scholars are mystified as to how mankind could universally obtain the idea that by killing some innocent life (*e.g.,* animals, babies, virgins, *etc.)* it would produce a beneficial result or supernatural favor. It all began in the Garden of Eden.

This is the great objective of God's incredible plan of redemption—the removal of sin so that the relationship with a holy God can be restored. By removing sin, the sinner is made holy (sanctification). As a result of being made holy, the penalty or price of death is paid and removed (justification). We are made righteous, and our spiritual relationship with a holy God is restored (reconciliation). God is not a God of anger and blood lust. He does not need blood to appease a superstitious appetite. Rather, blood atonement demonstrates to mankind the importance of His holiness and the seriousness of sin. Blood, representing life, is the only thing that will pay the price and atone for sin (Heb 9.22)—not good works, good beliefs, good morals, or good intentions. Blood (life) represents the highest price possible for the guilty party.

8

FAITH RESPONDS

Something is wrong. You go to the doctor. He runs tests and discovers that you have a life-threatening disease. He calls in a prescription of the medicine you need that will save your life. You obtain the medication and what do you do?

Do you take the medicine? If you have understood the doctor's instructions and you believed what the doctor has told you, you will take the medicine. What you have just experienced is belief in action, better known as faith.

What made animal sacrifice work? It derived its power from the faith of the believers. The followers of God understood His instructions and they believed that killing the animal would remove their sins. So they acted and performed the animal sacrifice according to the instructions God had given them. One couldn't just believe in animal sacrifice (Heb 9.22) any more than merely believing in medicine will make one well! The origin of true faith is, and always has been, by the instruction of God. Romans 10.17 emphasizes this point: *"Faith comes by hearing, and hearing by the word of God."*

Additionally, sacrificing without understanding *why*, would have been useless. Sacrifice derived no power from superstition, tradition, or ignorant obedience. Hebrews 11.6 defines genuine faith as having two elements—**belief** *and* **action:** *"**Without faith it is impossible to please Him,** for he who comes to God must **believe** that He is and that He is a rewarder of those who **diligently seek** Him."* Obedience from *the heart* is the type of faith that God has always desired. Here are some Old Testament examples of this type of faith as seen in Hebrews 11:

FAITH ACTS

*"By **faith** Abel **offered** unto God a more excellent sacrifice"*(v 4).
*"By **faith** Noah… moved with fear, **prepared** an ark"* (v 7).
*"By **faith** Abraham… **obeyed**… and **went** out"* (v 8).
*"By **faith** Abraham… **offered** up Isaac"* (v 17).

We see clearly that the kind of faith required by God is action based upon belief. Saving faith has always required this *belief-based action*. In the New Testament, James even asks rhetorically, *"Can such faith [without action] save a man?"* (Jas 2.14). James even points out that the devils themselves were all believers. If belief alone saved, then the devils would be saved! (Jas 2.14–26). Could a stronger argument against 'belief alone' be made?

Also, the removal of sin by animal sacrifice was a gift, not a work. If grandmother sends you a birthday check, you do not *earn* the gift because you endorse the check, take it to the bank, and have it cashed. Because you believed that grandmother had the funds in the bank you acted on faith and did the things you needed to do to *accept* her gift. When Old Testament persons sacrificed an animal they had done nothing to earn removal of sin. Because they believed God's promise of the removal of sin they were only accepting God's gracious gift (signing the check) when they sacrificed the animal. The action of obedient faith is not accomplishing some work that earns anything but is doing what God has told us to do to accept His gift. True faith is made complete by action (obedience) from the heart (belief).

9

Jesus is
God's Sacrificial Lamb

Several hundred years passed under the system of animal sacrifice. Then a climactic moment arrived. John was preaching, preparing the "way of the Lord." As Jesus approached him, John made an astounding public pronouncement that reverberates throughout history (John 1.29):

"Behold the lamb of God that takes away the sin of the world!"

There it is! The entire plan of redemption summarized in one sentence. By proclaiming Jesus as *"the lamb of God,"* John declared Jesus to be *God's* sacrifice to pay for the sins of humanity! *"You were not **redeemed** with perishable things like silver or gold… but with **precious blood, as of a lamb unblemished and spotless, the blood of Christ**"* (1 Pet 1.18). Notice these critical observations:

- **No Accidental Death.** Jesus' death was no accident or a failed mission to set up an earthly kingdom. His very purpose in coming to earth was to serve as a sacrifice. A sacrifice must die.
- **An Innocent Sacrifice.** If Jesus had ever sinned, even once, then He could not have been the lamb of God. He would have then had the price of death on His head for His sin and could not have served as a representative for you or me (1 John 3.5).
- **Removes Sins.** The result of being the "lamb of God" was that it would "take away the sin of the world." Sacrifice (of life) removes sin by payment of the judicial price of death.
- **Old Testament Fulfillment.** Christ is also referred to as our "Passover lamb" in 1 Corinthians 5.7: *"Get rid of the old yeast that you may be a new batch without yeast—as you really are. For Christ, our Passover lamb, has been sacrificed."* This is a reference to the blood of the lambs that were sacrificed, which was used to protect the Israelites from the angel of death in Egypt (Exod 12.3–49). Christ removed the "old yeast" (sin) from us by His sacrifice. In doing so He accomplished His purpose of fulfilling the Old Testament (Matt 5.17: *"Do not think that I came to abolish the Law or the Prophets; I did not come to abolish but to fulfill"*).

Jesus came to die, to take the place of animal sacrifice to fulfill the Old Testament (Matt 5.17). He came *"to give His life a ransom for many"* (Matt 20.28). *"For this is My **blood** of the covenant, which is **poured out for many for forgiveness**"* *of sins"* (Matt 26.28). *"You were **bought** with a **price"*** (1 Cor 7.23). Jesus paid the price of death—a payment humanity did not deserve—such is grace.

Christ's suffering and death was prophesied clearly, vividly, and specifically some 750 years earlier in Isaiah 53. Here is a sample:

> **5***But He was **pierced through for our transgressions,** He was **crushed for our iniquities;** The **chastening for our well-being fell upon Him, And by His scourging we are healed.** **6***All of us like sheep have gone astray, Each of us has turned to his own way; But the LORD has caused **the iniquity of us all To fall on Him.** **7***He was oppressed and He was afflicted, Yet He did not open His mouth; Like a lamb that is led to slaughter, And like a sheep that is silent before its shearers, So He did not open His mouth.* **8***By oppression and judgment He was taken away; And as for His generation, who considered That He was cut off out of the land of the living For the **transgression of my people, to whom the stroke was due?** **9***His grave was assigned with wicked men, Yet He was with a rich man in His death,* **Because He had done no violence,** *Nor was there any deceit in His mouth.* **10***But the Lord was pleased To crush Him, putting Him to grief; If He would render Himself as **a guilt offering,** He will see His offspring, He will prolong His days, And the good pleasure of the Lord will prosper in His hand.* **11***As a result of the anguish of His soul, He will see it and be satisfied; By His knowledge the Righteous One, My Servant, will **justify the many, As He will bear their iniquities.** **12***Therefore, I will allot Him a portion with the great, And He will divide the booty with the strong; Because He **poured out Himself to death**, And was numbered with the transgressors; Yet He Himself **bore the sin of many, And interceded for the transgressors.***

10

JESUS PAID THE PRICE OWED BY THE SINNER

Mel Gibson's famous movie *The Passion of the Christ* very graphically depicts the arrest, scourging, and crucifixion of Christ. What the movie does not explain is why Jesus went through the horrific scourging and subsequent ordeal of the cross. Why did Jesus have to have nails driven through His hands and a spear thrust through His side? Why did He have to die in the first place? The answer is now clear. Jesus suffered this ordeal and death on behalf of the sinner—*"to whom the stroke was due"* (Isa 53.8) and Jesus representatively took our place. He paid the price of suffering and death that was owed by each individual sinner. Jesus did indeed die for our sins. He did this by choice, out of love for His Father and His desire to do His will (Matt 26.42: *"Your will be done").*

By living a sinless life Jesus qualified Himself as an innocent stand-in to die in the place of the truly guilty—you and me. When Jesus died on the cross He took our sins upon Himself and paid the price of death owed by the sinner. *"He Himself bore our sins in His body on the cross, so that we might die to sin"* (1 Pet 2.24). Jesus died to sin on the cross so that we might die to sin (Rom 6.10–11) and be made righteous. In this manner, Christ's death *represents* the judicial death of the believer. This role of Christ is summed up in 2 Corinthians 5.21: *"He made **Him who knew no sin to be sin on our behalf**, so that **we might become** the righteousness of God in Him."* And in Hebrews 9.26–28: *"He has been manifested to **put away sin by the sacrifice of Himself**... having been offered once **to bear the sins of many**."*

Second Corinthians 5.14 says, *"One died on behalf of all, therefore all died."* L.A. Mott observed, "When He died, we all died. This conclusion could only be valid if that death on behalf of all was a death in place of all. The death of the Christ was for all. His death was our death. It satisfied the demand of the law for the death of each and every sinner."[1]

Jesus Christ, the Son of God, came to this earth as a man, so that as God and man, He could offer the perfect sacrifice, atone for our sins and reconcile man to God (Eph 2.13–16). First Corinthians 6.20 tells us, *"You have been bought with a price."* The price was Christ's death. All of us who are Christians are Christians because Christ paid the price of life that was owed. By dying with Christ, we share His victory over death and have hope of life eternal (1 Cor 1.30; see also Rom 4.25; 1 Pet 3.18; Heb 9.26–28; 2.17; 10.10; 13.12; Rom 5.6–10, 15; 3.23–25; 1 John 2.2; 3.5; 4.10; 2 Cor 5.17–19; Eph 2.11–16; Tit 2.14; Col 1.22; 1 Tim 2.5).

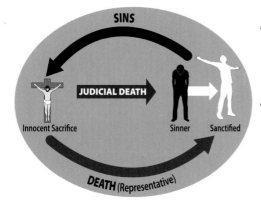

*"He Himself **bore our sins in His body** on the cross so that **we might die to sin"** (1 Pet 2.24).*

*"Our **old self was crucified with Him**... that our **body of sin might be done away** with"* (Rom 6.6).

---

[1]LA Mott, *Thinking Through Second Corinthians* (2002), 54.

11

THE RESURRECTION
PROVIDES PROOF AND POWER

Believing Jesus to have been a great moral teacher implies His teachings are true. Since He taught that He Himself is God, He logically must be God. The 35 miracles in the four gospels prove Jesus had powers beyond our human limitations. His miracles of nature provide strong confirmations of His divine claims. The hundreds of prophecies of the Messiah in the Old Testament were all fulfilled by Jesus of Nazareth, and that goes far beyond coincidence.

Not to diminish the importance of this evidence, but all claims of Jesus stand or fall with His resurrection. Without the resurrection, His claim to be the Son of God—that is, deity in human flesh—vanishes into thin air. Without the resurrection His death as payment for our sins is meaningless. Without the resurrection we are wasting our time.

The importance of the resurrection was immediately recognized by the apostles, and we find statement after statement in the New Testament emphasizing the importance of Jesus' full and complete victory over death. In the words of Paul:

If there is no resurrection of the dead, then not even Christ has been raised. And if Christ has not been raised, our preaching is useless and so is your faith. More than that, we are then found to be false witnesses about God, for we have testified about God that he raised Christ from the dead. But he did not raise him if in fact the dead are not raised. For if the dead are not raised, then Christ has not been raised either. And if Christ has not been raised, your faith is futile; you are still in your sins. Then those also who have fallen asleep in Christ are lost. If only for this life we have hope in Christ, we are to be pitied more than all men. But Christ has indeed been raised from the dead, the first fruits of those who have fallen asleep. (1 Cor 15.13–22)

The resurrection is the ultimate miracle provided for us by God in order to prove beyond any dispute that Jesus is indeed the Son of God. No one in history successfully claimed to have resurrected himself from death. Nor does any other world religion claim a miracle such as the resurrection, or anything even near this magnitude.[2] Respected Christian scholar William Lane Craig writes:

Without the belief in the resurrection the Christian faith could not have come into being. The disciples would have remained crushed and defeated men. Even had they continued to remember Jesus as their beloved teacher,

---

[2]Rob van de Weghe, *Prepared to Answer*, (2007), 233.

His crucifixion would have forever silenced any hopes of His being the Messiah. The cross would have remained the sad and shameful end of His career. The origin of Christianity therefore hinges on the belief of the early disciples that God had raised Jesus from the dead. [3]

When Christ died, His followers thought it was all over and acted cowardly. They hid from others and publicly denied that they even knew Him. But when they saw the risen Christ, cowardice gave way to courage and these same men boldly proclaimed Him. Eventually all suffered a martyr's death (with the possible exception of John) due to their conviction that Christ had returned from the dead! *"Who [Christ], was **declared the Son of God with power by the resurrection from the dead"*** (Rom 1.4). No one will die for what he knows is a lie.

Christ was dead and buried; His resurrection three days later proved His claims to divinity. Acts 17.31 says, *"He has fixed a day in which He will judge the world in righteousness through a Man whom He has appointed, having **furnished proof to all men by raising Him from the dead."***

First Corinthians 15.1–8 succinctly summarizes the gospel message:

> *Now I make known to you, brethren, **the gospel** which I preached to you, which also you received, in which also you stand, by which also you are saved, if you hold fast the word which I preached to you, unless you believed in vain. For I delivered to you as of first importance what I also received, that **Christ died for our sins** according to the Scriptures, and that **He was buried,** and that **He was raised** on the third day according to the Scriptures, and that **He appeared** to Cephas, then to the twelve. After that He appeared to more than five hundred brethren at one time… and last of all, as to one untimely born, He appeared to me also.*

The phrase *"Christ died for our sins"* sums up the entire plan of redemption and the rest of this passage shows the importance of Christ's resurrection and subsequent appearances as foundational elements to the gospel message.

12

THE BELIEVER MUST DIE WITH CHRIST

This is the primary purpose of the plan of redemption—that the believer dies through and with his representative, Jesus Christ. Christ's death represents the

---

[3]William Lane Craig, *Knowing the Truth About the Resurrection* (1988), 116.

death of the believer. This is required in order to remove sin. It should come as no surprise to find that Christians are represented in the New Testament as those who, in the past, have died with Christ. For example:

"*If* **we died with Him** *we will also live with Him*" (2 Tim 2.11). Notice that the Christian is one who has died *with* Christ, not *for* Christ, or *in* Christ, or *because* of Christ, but *with* Christ. The believer must die with Christ, because that is the only way the judicial price for sin can be paid. The entire purpose of Christ coming to earth to be the lamb of God was so that believers could die with Him, have their sins removed, and be reconciled to a holy God. You and I should recognize that this is indeed "good news" and be willing to accept the wonderful gift of the lamb of God. It should also be clear why God would react with wrath toward anyone that would reject the gift of His son. Note also:

- "*Since* **you died with Christ**" (Col 2.20; see Rom 6.8).
- "**You have died** *and your life is hidden with Christ*" (Col 3.3).
- "*I have been* **crucified with Christ**" (Gal 2.20; see 2 Cor 5.14; Rom 6.7).

Note three facts about these passages:
1. They are addressed to Christians—those presently in Christ.
2. This terminology refers to the point in time past when one actually became a Christian.
3. The Christian is represented as one who has died with Christ.

It must also be clear that believers will not have any sin forgiven *unless* they have *died to sin;* they have *died with Christ;* they have been *united with Christ in His death;* and they have been *crucified with Christ.*

So, What is the Question?

Suppose that you have just heard this gospel message for the first time—that God is holy, sin separates you from Him, the price of death is on your head to pay for sin, and that Jesus came to pay the price for you, and that by dying with Him you can have your sins removed, and be reconciled to a holy God. If you believed this good news, what question would come to mind at this point? If this is the gospel message—that Christ dies for (in place of) the sinner—the believer must ask, "*How,* or *when* do I die with Christ?" "*How,* or *when* does this happen for me?"

At what point in my faith do I:
    Die to sin?
    Die with Christ?

When or How does God view me as:
    Uniting with Christ in his death?
    Being crucified with Christ?

There are many different answers to these four questions offered by many different religious groups. That's because, just as Galatians 1 warned us, there are different gospels being propagated by different professing Christians.

We Must Have a Bible Answer to These Crucial Questions

We must know the Bible's answer to these questions, not just the opinions of man. The answers to these questions is the response to the one gospel.

Answers to our four questions are clearly and specifically given in Romans 6. Christians in Rome had developed a misconception about God's grace. Some apparently thought that once they had their sins removed and became Christians they could then sin all they wanted to, and the grace of God would only increase all the more. It is in the context of addressing this erroneous idea that our four questions are answered. Take a look at the key verses in Romans 6, and pay particular attention to the prepositions:

*¹What shall we say then? Are we to continue in sin so that grace may increase? ²May it never be! How shall **we who died to sin** still live in it?* Imagine using the grace of God as a license to sin! First, he reminds them that they had died to sin. One of our questions: "When do I die to sin?" is answered clearly in the next verse:

*³Or do you not know that **all of us who have been baptized into Christ Jesus** have been baptized into His death?* Here our 'When and How' question is answered clearly and specifically. We died to sin when we were baptized into Christ—when we were baptized into His death. This is the purpose of baptism. It is the act of faith that puts us into Christ by placing us into Christ's death—the entire purpose of His work on earth! Paul reminded them that when they died with Christ, they entered into His death. If you could get into anyone's death, you would be dead. Why do I need to get "into Christ's death?" Because Christ paid the judicial price for sin (death) and I must pay that same price by dying with Him—by being placed into His death.

*⁴Therefore **we have been buried with Him through baptism into death,** so that as Christ was raised from the dead through the glory of the Father, so we too might walk in **newness of life.*** Two very important truths are here. First, when you are baptized into Christ—when you are baptized into His death—you are buried with Christ into death. Secondly, the result is a new life! Why? Because when you die with Christ your sins are removed. This is elsewhere referred to as the *"new birth"* or becoming a *"new creation"* (John 3.3; 2 Cor 5.17) or as Romans 6 says, we receive *"newness of life."*

*⁵For if **we have become united with Him in the likeness of His death,** certainly we shall also be in the likeness of His resurrection.* Precisely when are you united with Christ in the likeness of His death? When you are baptized into Christ and into His death, you are then united with Christ's death so that your sins can be removed by the price of His death.

6*Knowing this, that* **our old self was crucified with Him,** *in order that our body of sin might be done away with, so that we would no longer be slaves to sin.* Precisely when does God consider you crucified with Christ? When you are baptized into Christ, you are baptized into His death. It is as if you were on the cross with Him, paying the price for your sins! The result is that "[y]our body of sin" is done away with at this point, by uniting with His death.

7*For* **he who has died is freed from sin.** When does the sinner die? When you are baptized into Christ—when you are baptized into His death. What is the result? You and I are then freed from sin—our sins are removed, forgiven by the judicial price of death being paid.

8*Now if* **we have died with Christ,** *we believe that we shall also live with Him,* **9***knowing that Christ, having been raised from the dead, is never to die again; death no longer is master over Him.* When does God view you as dying with Christ? When you are baptized into Christ—when you are baptized into His death. Don't let the importance of this verse escape you. The entire purpose of Christ coming to earth to be the sacrificial Lamb of God and pay the judicial price of sin was so that you could die *with* Him, have your sins removed, and be reconciled to a Holy God.

10*For the death that He died,* **He died to sin** *once for all; but the life that He lives, He lives to God.* **11***Even so consider* **yourselves to be dead to sin,** *but alive to God in Christ Jesus.* Just as Christ "died to sin" by literally dying and thus paying the judicial price for sin, we are to also consider ourselves "to be dead to sin" by dying with Christ, thus having paid the judicial price for sin (1 Pet 2.24). When? How? When you are baptized into Christ—when you are baptized into His death.

12*Therefore* **do not let sin reign in your mortal body** *so that you obey its lusts,* **13***and do not go on presenting the members of your body to sin as instruments of unrighteousness; but present yourselves to God* **as those alive from the dead,** *and your members as instruments of righteousness to God.* **14***For sin shall not be master over you, for you are not under law but under grace.* Now we get the stated purpose for the entire previous discourse—stop sinning! Now that you have died with Christ and your sins were removed, you should have a different attitude toward sin. A parent finds one of their children playing in the mud, hoses them off, brings them in, gives them a bath, dresses them in fresh clothes, and then sternly tells them, "Don't go get dirty again!" Similarly, Paul is saying that you have been extracted out of the muck of the world and been cleaned up by the blood of Christ, don't crawl back into the mud—don't go get dirty again! By reminding the Romans of what

Christ had done for them when they were baptized into Christ and His death, they should understand that they should no longer want to sin or be slaves to sin. This is the idea of repentance—that a Christian must have a changed attitude toward sin. Repentance plays an important role in the plan of redemption. Without repentance, baptism will be of no use. Rather than sinning more we must do just the opposite, and stop practicing sin (1 John 3.4–9).

[17]*But thanks be to God that though you were slaves of sin,* **you became obedient from the heart** *to that form of teaching to which you were committed.* Here he reminded them that it was by faith (action = "obedient" plus belief = "from the heart") that they were saved. Baptism derives no power from the water, superstition, or meritorious work. It derives its power solely from the faith of the participant. The sinner learns of the work of Christ to remove sin, believes it, and now participates in the death of Christ to have his or her sins removed. Our hearts are cleansed by faith when we are baptized.

[22]*But now having been* **freed from sin** *and enslaved to God, you derive your benefit, resulting in* **sanctification**, *and* **the outcome, eternal life.** As a result they were freed from sin, and their sins removed. As a result of having been baptized into Christ and His death and having their sins removed they were made holy, sanctified. As 1 Corinthians 6.11 states: *"Such were some of you; but you were* **washed**, *but you were* **sanctified**, *but you were* **justified** *in the name of the Lord Jesus Christ and in the*

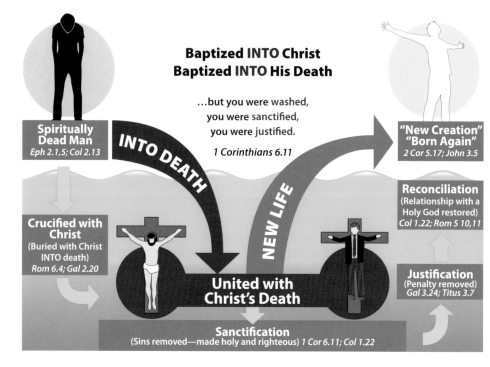

Baptized INTO Christ
Baptized INTO His Death

…but you were washed,
you were sanctified,
you were justified.

1 Corinthians 6.11

Spiritually Dead Man
Eph 2.1,5; Col 2.13

INTO DEATH

"New Creation"
"Born Again"
2 Cor 5.17; John 3.5

Reconciliation
(Relationship with a Holy God restored)
Col 1.22; Rom 5 10,11

Crucified with Christ
(Buried with Christ INTO death)
Rom 6.4; Gal 2.20

NEW LIFE

United with Christ's Death

Justification
(Penalty removed)
Gal 3.24; Titus 3.7

Sanctification
(Sins removed—made holy and righteous) *1 Cor 6.11; Col 1.22*

Spirit of our God." Sanctification results in justification (the price of death is paid and removed) which reconciles us to a holy God.

²³*For the wages of sin is death, but **the free gift of God is eternal life** in Christ Jesus our Lord.* After this great explanation of what we experience by accepting God's grace when we are baptized into Christ, the Romans are reminded that this was a free gift of God. Being baptized into Christ and into His death had not earned God's grace or mercy, they had only accepted the cleansing power of Christ's death by faith as a gift.

Baptism is the point where your sins are cleansed by faith in Christ's blood—where you die with Christ. As such, baptism is *when* you are united with Christ's death by faith and, as a result, this is the moment *when* your sins are removed and you are sanctified, justified, and made righteous (1 Cor 6.11) before God.

We will now examine four testimonies from the New Testament and history that validate this message and provide further evidence that what was examined in Section One is indeed *the* gospel message.

SECTION TWO

FOUR TESTIMONIES

But now a righteousness from God, apart from law, has been made known, to which the Law and the Prophets testify. This righteousness from God comes through faith in Jesus Christ to all who believe. There is no difference, for all have sinned and fall short of the glory of God, and are justified freely by his grace through the redemption that came by Christ Jesus. God presented him as a sacrifice of atonement, through faith in his blood. He did this to demonstrate his justice, because in his forbearance he had left the sins committed beforehand unpunished— he did it to demonstrate his justice at the present time, so as to be just and the one who justifies those who have faith in Jesus.

Romans 3.21-26

Therefore, since we are surrounded by such a great cloud of witnesses, let us throw off everything that hinders and the sin that so easily entangles, and let us run with perseverance the race marked out for us. Let us fix our eyes on Jesus, the author and perfecter of our faith, who for the joy set before him endured the cross, scorning its shame, and sat down at the right hand of the throne of God.

Hebrews 12.1–2

13
What the Apostles Taught

First we will examine the testimony to this response to the gospel message in some of the teachings of the apostles themselves. The apostles were given all authority by Jesus (Matt 16.19) and were inspired by the Holy Spirit on the day of Pentecost just as Jesus had promised them so that they would have all truth (John 16.13). The apostles taught that baptism was the point *when* (or *how):*

- **We are *justified by faith*** (Gal 3.26–27). Justification, in its most literal sense, carries the idea of aligning something. For example, when we type and right-justify our text we align our text on the right. In a spiritual sense our sins have put us out of "alignment" with God. The only way to be brought back into alignment, or justified, is to have our sins removed. Justification, therefore, is the legal equivalent of being pronounced "not guilty" by a judge. When our sins are removed the price of death is removed (justification). We learned previously from Romans 6.17 that faith is the active component in baptism when our sins are removed. This is why, in Galatians 3.27, we are reminded that at the moment we put on Christ in baptism, we are "justified by faith" (3.24) or become "sons of God by faith" (3.26). It is important to note that when God performs justification of sinners he is not declaring us to be "good", or saying that we were not sinners after all. He is pronouncing us *legally righteous,* free from the condemnation of the law because His Son has paid the price for our law-breaking.

- **We are *saved by faith* in Christ's work** (Col 2.12). We are *"buried with Him in baptism,"* and *"raised up with Him through faith in the working of God."* Baptism is not a meritorious work that earns salvation. It is simply the point where we *accept* God's promise—and *His* work. Therefore we are *buried with Christ* when we are immersed in water and *raised up with Christ through faith* in the ***working of God.*** This again places the emphasis on the role of faith that saves us when we believe in what Christ has done for us and respond to that by dying with Him in baptism. We also observe the symbolism of baptism in this passage in the representation of Christ's death, burial, and resurrection reenacted in immersion.

- **We are saved** (1 Pet 3.21). Here Peter flatly states *"Baptism now saves you."* Does this mean that we don't need to believe, confess Jesus' name, or repent of our sins? Of course not. This is a figure of speech called synecdoche, where a part is used to represent the whole. This passage further explains *how* baptism saves. First, through faith, the *"an appeal to God for a good conscience."* Faith in what? In the working of God *("through the resurrection of Christ").* This passage is a parallel to Colossians 2.12.

- **When we are sanctified** (Eph 5.25–27). Here we learn that Christ gave himself up for the church so that he could sanctify the church. How? *"Having cleansed her by the **washing of water** with the word, that He might present to Himself the church in all her glory, having no spot or wrinkle or any such thing; but that she would be holy and blameless."* The church was made holy and blameless (sanctified) when people were baptized (washing of water).

- **We are renewed** (Tit 3.3–5). Here we are taught that *"He saved us, not on the basis of deeds which we have done in righteousness, but according to His mercy, by the washing of regeneration and renewing by the Holy Spirit."* We learn that salvation occurs as a result of the regeneration and renewing that is effected by the Holy Spirit *when* we are baptized. We see the role of the Holy Spirit in sanctification by the actual *removal* of our sins, elsewhere referred to as *"the sanctifying work of the Spirit"* (1 Pet 1.2). Second Thessalonians 2.13 ties this directly to our faith, *"God has chosen you from the beginning for salvation through **sanctification** by the Spirit and **faith** in the truth."* In the 'washing' of baptism, it could be said that the Holy Spirit does the actual 'scrubbing' (removal of sin) and presents us back to God as holy and clean, renewed, regenerated—a new birth, a new creation (2 Cor. 5.17). This occurs *when* we are baptized and is accomplished by *our faith* in the working of God (Col 2.1–12). We are also reminded again that this is not accomplished by anything we have done but according to God's mercy.

Not By Works

When we are baptized into Christ and into His death we merely accept the gift of God's mercy by faith. We do not perform a righteous work. Baptism is just a means of accepting the gift (signing the check). We *accept* God's gift of grace and mercy when we respond by faith to what Christ did for us (Rom 6.23, Tit 3.5). Baptism is not a righteous work that earns anything! It is merely *the* act of faith by which we accept the work of Christ and God's promise to remove our sins and restore our relationship to Him (1 Pet 3.21; Rom 6.23; Tit 3.5–7). We could never have our sins removed on the basis of something we ourselves performed or accomplished! (Eph 2.8–9).

Let's also be clear that there is nothing in the water that removes sin. Likewise, a bull, goat, or lamb cannot take away sin. While their sins were forgiven at the time of sacrifice (Lev 16.30) we learn from Hebrews 10.4,11 what is rather obvious to us now—it was neither priestly ritual nor the blood of bulls and goats that removed sin. Nothing that is on or of this earth has any power to remove sin, not animals, ritual, good works, or water for that matter. The sins forgiven under the first covenant were removed by the sacrifice of Christ (Heb 9.15). Christ's blood transcends time and space. It is on the basis of His sacrifice, and His alone, that any sin would ever be forgiven. God forgave the sins in the Old Testament on the basis of the surety of His plan and purpose in the plan of redemption which had existed before He even created the universe (Eph 1.4). Christ is portrayed as being slain "from the foundation of the world." (1 Pet 1.20; Rev 13.8). God had planned or purposed it, He would surely make it come to pass, just as he described things He had planned in Isaiah as already happened. "Have you not heard? Long ago I did it, from ancient times I planned it. Now I have brought it to pass" (Isa 37.26; 46.10–11). All the sins of history, all the sins of the present, and all of the sins that will be committed and forgiven are, and will be, forgiven solely on the basis of Christ's sacrifice. Again, 1 Peter 3.18, "For Christ also died for sins once for all, the just for the unjust, so that He might bring us to God."

At this point it may seem that there is an unusual emphasis being placed on the act and action of baptism. One reason for this emphasis is that over time, particularly since the Reformation, most religious groups have denigrated the role of baptism to either superstition, pure symbolism, or, at worst, a peculiar church tradition, certainly not an integral component of saving faith or necessary in any sense. Another reason for this emphasis is that the New Testament places a significant emphasis on its role as well.

The New Testament Emphasis on Baptism, Ephesians 4.4–6

Here is an important list of seven truths upon which all Christians *must* be unified *("keep the unity of the Spirit in the bond of peace")*—one body, one spirit, one hope, one Lord, one faith, one God and Father, and *one baptism. Why* is baptism on this list? Many things important to Christian faith aren't on this list. If baptism is just some fuzzy, symbolic action that is of no necessity then why would it be on a list like this? If we understand the connection that Romans 6 makes in connecting baptism to the death of Christ then we can understand both its importance and necessity. Baptism is on this list because it is *the* act of faith, and *the* point at which one's sins are removed by dying with Christ.

Just as there is only *one* gospel, there is only *one* baptism. The fact that there is only *one* baptism further attests to its importance and connection with the *one gospel* of Galatians 1. When this was written by Paul there were many baptisms that existed. There were Jewish ceremonial washings, there was John's baptism, there was baptism of the Holy Spirit (in at least three instances), there were those baptizing for the dead, and so on.

When Paul arrived in Ephesus he found some claiming to be disciples. He realized that they had not received the promised Holy Spirit and consequently these "disciples" were not true Christians. At this point he asked the single clearest question he could ask in order to determine what the problem was, *"So Paul asked, 'Then what baptism did you receive?' 'John's baptism,' they replied."* (Acts 19.1–7) Why would Paul bother to ask about their baptism if it was of no importance? After explaining to the Ephesians why John's baptism was inadequate, they were *re-baptized.* The fact that they had been previously immersed was of no benefit when done for the wrong reason.

We have many baptisms floating around today also: infant baptism, baptism to join a church, baptism to show commitment, baptism as a work of obedience, some claim Holy Spirit baptism, baptism by proxy, and so on. Yet Paul says there is only one baptism. This is another "one" that can't be compromised, just like one God or one gospel. How can we be sure of this one baptism? Wouldn't it be great if we had somewhere we could find actual examples of conversion to compare with the many practices we see today? That is exactly what we have in the book of Acts—actual historical examples.

14

WHAT THE APOSTLES PRACTICED

Examples of what the apostles actually practiced are very powerful and valuable. We should be willing to test our theological beliefs against actual examples. The book of Acts is a book of history, documenting the events surrounding the establishment of the church and the execution of the Great Commission. In the following examples from the book of Acts we can see very clearly that baptism was:

- *Commanded* "For Remission of Sins" (Acts 2.38). After hearing Peter preach the first gospel sermon on the Day of Pentecost, the *believers* specifically asked, *"What must we do?"* They could have been given many popular answers that we hear today—"just believe" or "just accept Jesus into your heart" or "pray the sinner's prayer"—but instead they were commanded to repent and be baptized *for* (in order to obtain) the remission of sins.
- *Included* in "Preaching the Gospel" (Acts 8.5, 12). Here Philip proclaimed *the gospel.* When they believed, they were being baptized. Preaching the one gospel *must* have included instruction about the baptismal response.
- *Included* in "Preaching Jesus" (Acts 8.35–39). Here Philip *"preached Jesus"* (the one gospel) to the eunuch, and his immediate reaction was to inquire about being baptized. Preaching Jesus *had* to include instruction about baptism. He rejoiced only *after* the two men both *"went down into the water"* and

he was baptized. Notice also that an angel of the Lord sent Philip to the chariot. This is because, as we saw earlier, the gospel is a spoken message and the Eunuch needed to *hear* the gospel (he did not have a New Testament with him as yet!) in order to believe it and respond to it by faith.

- **When and Where** *the Lord Added* **"To the Church"** (Acts 2.47). After being baptized *("those being saved")* the *Lord* added them to His church, His spiritual kingdom, where Christ is king (see also Eph 5.25–27, Col 1.18). The church is nothing more than a collection of those that have been sanctified by having their sins removed in baptism (Eph 5.25–27).

The One Baptism
From just a couple of examples in Acts 2 and Acts 8 we can find some clear markers as to what constituted the "one baptism":

- *One Candidate.* Only believers were commanded to be baptized. That is because, as we have seen earlier, baptism is an act of faith. Infants cannot have faith. Infant baptism is an act of superstition, not faith.
- *One Mode.* We see from Acts 8 that baptism was immersion in water. The word *baptism* in Greek literally means *immersion*. Baptism requires immersion because it symbolizes the death, burial, and resurrection of Jesus and the believer's uniting with the same. This is why other modes of baptism, *e.g.*, sprinkling, pouring, *etc.* are not the one baptism of Ephesians 4.
- *One Purpose.* From Acts 2 we learn that baptism, when following belief, confession, and repentance, was for remission of sins. The Greek is very specific here using the word *eis* for the word *for*. *Eis* literally means "in order to," implying one thing results in the other. A parallel construction would be found in Matthew 26.28: *"For this is My blood of the covenant, which is poured out for many for (Gk. "eis") forgiveness of sins."* Baptism done for any other reason or purpose is not the one baptism of Ephesians 4.
- *One Result.* From Acts 2 we also see that those who were baptized were added to the church. This is because, as we saw from Ephesians 5, that the church is composed of those that have been sanctified. No one is in the kingdom until after he or she has been made holy by putting on Christ in the one baptism.
- *One Directive.* We further see from Acts 2 that the one baptism was commanded of believers. This would rule out baptism of the Holy Spirit as the one baptism for it was never commanded of believers, but was only promised and experienced by a few. Furthermore, if we understand what Romans 6 is telling us—that baptism is when and how we die with Christ and have our sins removed—we can truly appreciate why it is commanded.

The Example of the Conversion of Paul
One of the clearest examples of conversion in the New Testament is that of the

apostle Paul (Acts 9; 22). With a clear conscience and great sincerity he persecuted Christians, confident he was doing the will of God. When Paul traveled to Damascus, Christ appeared to him in a vision and directed him to go into the city *"where you will be told what you must do."* We see several key elements of Paul's repentance:

- He **believed** and **confessed**—*"What must I do, **Lord?**"*
- He **obeyed**—*"Get up and go into Damascus."*
- He **fasted** for three days—*"Three days… and neither ate nor drank."*
- He **prayed** for three days—*"For he is praying."*

Do you think Paul prayed "the sinner's prayer"? The words of Paul's prayer are not recorded, but we must believe it to be a prayer of repentance that would rival David's own prayer of repentance in Psalm 51. Paul had just become a believer in Jesus and had learned that all those Christians he had been persecuting were children of God! I can only imagine the pain, suffering, and repentance that were reflected in his prayers.

Paul also was the recipient of a miraculous healing as Ananias miraculously restored his sight (Acts 22.12).

The question is often asked, "When was Paul saved?" At what point in these three days of repentance were his sins removed? When he believed? Confessed? Obeyed? Fasted? Healed? Through his earnest penitent praying? The sum answer is, "No."

Ananias, instructed by God to go to Paul, commanded him, *"Now why do you delay? Get up and **be baptized**, and **wash away your sins**, calling on His name"* (Acts 22.16). Until Ananias baptized him, Paul was still full of sin. None of Paul's acts of repentance or obedience had removed a single sin. Why? Because he had not yet died with Christ. He still needed to have his sins "washed away" in baptism. There is a strong lesson here for all of us. Whether we have believed, confessed, prayed, or otherwise repented for three days, three months, three years, or 30 years, the only way to remove sin is to "die with Christ" by uniting with His atoning death that pays the judicial price for our sins.

Identifying the One Baptism of Ephesians 4.4–6

One Candidate: Believers, Acts 2.38; **One Purpose:** For Remission of Sins, Acts 2.38; **One Mode:** Immersion in Water, Acts 8.36–38; **One Result:** Entrance into the Kingdom, Acts 2.47; **One Directive:** Commanded, Acts 2.38, Matthew 28.19

---

[4]*The Epistle of Barnabas,* Chapter 11, verses 8–11, Roberts-Donaldson. This epistle, while most likely not written by the well-known Barnabas of the New Testament, reflects an accurate picture of the early Christian belief and practice regarding baptism.

15

THE BELIEF AND PRACTICE
OF THE EARLY CHURCH

Testimony of the Early Church

The early church *universally* believed, taught, and practiced that baptism was when our sins are removed by faith. Many first century writers trained directly at the feet of the apostles. The Epistle of Barnabas (AD 70), for example, says,

> Blessed are they who, **placing their trust in the cross,** have **gone down in the water.** …We indeed descend into the water **full of sins** and defilement. However, we come up, bearing fruit in our heart, having **the fear of God and the trust of Jesus in our spirit.**[4]

This epistle reflects a common understanding that baptism was that point when one's faith cleansed him from sin. Such quotations can be replicated over and over from the writings of early church leaders. Here are just a few examples:

> There is no other way [to obtain God's blessings] than this—to become acquainted with Christ, to be washed in the fountain spoken of by Isaiah for the remission of sins. (ca. AD 110–165)[5]

And also,

> And for this rite we have learned from the apostles this reason… in order that we may not remain the children of necessity and of ignorance, but may become the children of choice and knowledge, and may obtain in the water the remission of sins formerly committed, there is pronounced over him who chooses to be born again, and has repented of his sins, the name of God the Father and Lord of the universe. (ca. AD 110–165)[6]

> Baptism itself is a corporal act by which we are plunged into the water, while its effect is spiritual, in that we are freed from our sins. (ca. AD 140–230)[7]

> Being baptized, we are illuminated; illuminated, we become sons; being made sons, we are made perfect; being made perfect, we are made immortal. …This work is variously called grace, and illumination, and perfection, and washing. Washing, by which we cleanse away our sins; grace, by which the penalties accruing to transgressions are remitted; and illumination, by

---

[5]Justin Martyr, *Trypho* chap. 44.

[6]Justin Martyr, "First Apology," *Ante-Nicene Fathers,* vol. 1, pg. 183.

[7]Tertullian, "On Baptism," *Ante-Nicene Fathers,* vol. 3, page 670).

which that holy light of salvation is beheld, that is, by which we see God clearly." (ca. AD 150–215)[8]

David Bercot observed,

In short, baptism in early Christianity was the supernatural rite of initiation by which a new believer passed from being the old man of the flesh to being a newly reborn man of the spirit. However, please don't think their practice was some empty ritual. The early Christians didn't separate baptism from faith and repentance. Baptism wasn't some magical ritual that could regenerate a person if it wasn't accompanied by faith and repentance. They specifically taught that God was under no necessity to grant forgiveness of sins simply because a person went through the motions of baptism. A faithless person was not reborn through water baptism.[9]

Who could better understand the gospel taught by the apostles: those who were taught directly by the apostles and worked with them, or theologians over fifteen hundred years later? Indeed, the early church believed, taught and practiced the same gospel taught and practiced by the apostles themselves.

16

WHAT JESUS COMMANDED

How important are the actual words and commands of Jesus? What did Jesus Himself teach? Now revisit Jesus' command to His followers in the Great Commission as He is about to depart the earth: *"Go into all the world and **preach the gospel** to every creature. He that **believes and is baptized will be saved,** he that does not believe will be condemned"* (Mark 16.5–16, also Matt 28.19). Understanding God's plan of redemption, we can see why *Christ commanded baptism* for those who *believed* the gospel, and why belief in the gospel is a *prerequisite* to baptism and salvation. Also notice that the power of the *spoken* gospel message was what was to be used to generate faith (Rom 10.17; 1.16).

Belief Alone?

What about passages such as John 3.16 that seem to indicate Jesus was teaching that everyone who believes (mental assent only) will be saved. "Believe" in this and other passages is, as stated earlier, synecdoche—a figure of speech where

---

[8]Clement of Alexandria, "The Instructor," *Ante-Nicene Fathers,* vol. 2, pg. 215.

[9]David W. Bercot, *Will the Real Heretics Please Stand Up?* (Scroll Publishing, 1989), p 80.

a part represents the whole (*e.g.,* "head" for a cow; "sail" for a sailboat, *etc.).* In these passages, *belief* is used as synecdoche, where the part (belief) is used to represent *all* that is involved in salvation; *e.g.,* confession, repentance, baptism. As we saw earlier in 1 Peter 3.21, Peter flatly states, *"Baptism now saves you."* If similarly taken out of context, then 1 Peter 3.21 would teach that a person doesn't even need to believe! This is also synecdoche where baptism represents *all* that a person does to accept God's gift of salvation—believe, repent, and confess. Belief is often used in the New Testament as synecdoche, to represent the entire process of acceptance of the gift of salvation, just as baptism is so used in 1 Peter 3.21. A clear example of this is seen in the conversion of the Philippian jailor in Acts 16. Here *"they spoke the word of the Lord [the gospel] to him together with all who were in his house. And he took them that very hour of the night and washed their wounds, and immediately he was baptized, he and all his household. And he brought them into his house and set food before them, and rejoiced greatly, having **believed** in God with his whole household"* (Acts 16.32–34). In this passage we see the entire process of hearing the gospel message and responding to it in baptism referred to as "having believed in God."

Institution of the New Covenant

Jesus, while on earth as God incarnate, certainly had the ability to forgive sins and did so on a few occasions. A famous example is the thief on the cross (Luke 23.43). But notice that *after* Christ's sacrifice and death on the cross, His burial, and resurrection, He *commanded* His followers to extend salvation to humanity on the basis of their faith *in His death, burial, and resurrection* (Mark 16.5–16).

Jesus also lived under the Law of Moses. The Law of Moses died on the cross with Jesus (Eph 2.14–16; Col 2.14). On the Day of Pentecost the Apostles, having just received the promised outpouring of the Holy Spirit, established His church. God's grace in redemption was now extended, not on the basis of the Law of Moses but on the sacrifice of Christ. Just as Jesus had commanded them in the great commission, the apostles commanded the believers to *"repent and be baptized for the remission of your sins."* (Acts 2.38) We would be presumptuous at best and condemned at worst (Gal 1.5–9) to extend God's grace on any other basis (or gospel).

Water and Spirit

Jesus further commanded in John 3.5 *"Unless one is **born of water and the Spirit**, he cannot enter into the kingdom of God."* This is one of the strongest baptismal commands in the New Testament. The parallel passage in Titus 3.5 reads, *"He saved us… according to His mercy, by the **washing of regeneration and renewing by the Holy Spirit.**"* As discussed earlier, we see the role of the Holy Spirit in the actual removal of our sins, elsewhere referred to as *"the sanctifying work of the Spirit"*

(1 Pet 1.2; 2 Thes 2.13). This occurs when we are baptized and it is accomplished by *our faith* in the working of God (Col 2.1–12).

Irenaeus, a disciple of Polycarp who had been taught personally by the apostle John, wrote the following in AD 150.

> As we are lepers in sin, we are made clean from our transgressions by means of the sacred water and the invitation of the Lord. We are thus spiritually regenerated as newborn infants, even as the Lord declared, *"Except a man be born again through water and the Spirit, he shall not enter into the kingdom of heaven."* (John 3.3)[10]

Early Christians used John 3.3–5 as their baptismal proof text! They clearly understood Jesus to be speaking of the new birth that occurs when one is baptized in water and is renewed by the work of the Holy Spirit in sanctification.

William Wall remarked in his general observations about baptism,

> All the ancient Christians (without the exception of one man) do understand that rule of the Savior, John 3.5… all that mention that text, from Justin Martyr down to Augustine do so apply it. Neither did I ever see it otherwise applied in any ancient writer. I believe Calvin was the first that ever denied this place to mean baptism. He gives another interpretation, which he confesses to be new.[11]

Making Disciples

Finally, Jesus, in a parallel account of the Great Commission, further commanded His followers to *"Go therefore and make disciples of all the nations, baptizing them in the name of the Father and the Son and the Holy Spirit, teaching them to observe all that I commanded you; and lo, I am with you always, even to the end of the age"* (Matt 28.19–20). Observe that Jesus here again commands that His disciples would be created by being baptized in the name of—or by the authority of—the Father, Son, and Holy Spirit. They are also to be taught to *"observe all that I commanded you."*

There is no doubt where supreme authority in His kingdom resides, for God has given it to His risen Son. *"All authority has been given to me,"* Christ said, *"in heaven and on earth"* (Matt 28.18). So how does Jesus Christ exercise His authority and rule his church today? The apostles were given the authority of Christ while they were here on earth (John 14.26; Matt 16.19; 1 Thes 2.6) and delivered the faith once for all (Jude 1.3; 2 Pet 1.3). This forms the basis for having the authority of Christ, as delivered by the apostles, for all of the work and worship of Christ's church. Christ exercises His authority today by His Spirit through His word.

---

[10]Irenaeus, "Fragments From Lost Writings", no. 34, *Ante-Nicene Fathers,* vol. 1, pg. 574.

[11]William Wall, "The History of Infant Baptism", Vol. 1, pg. 443.

When we are baptized into Christ we are added to His kingdom. Who is the king? Jesus Christ is the king. Does it matter to the king how He is worshipped? Does it matter to the king what kind of work is done in His kingdom? The scepter by which Christ rules His kingdom is His word delivered in scripture. It is only common sense to realize that what we observe the church in the New Testament performing by example and command was done by the direct authority of the apostles, just as Christ had commanded them. True disciples of Christ will not only be created by being baptized into Christ but will also make every attempt to follow apostolic authority in all of their work and worship because it reflects the glory and honor to be given to the king of the kingdom, Jesus Christ.

17

Summary

The overarching purpose of the Bible is not to teach facts of science or history. It is a message from God to communicate to His creation the facts of salvation. Through carefully orchestrated events, all of history unfolds to reveal the divine plan of redemption: God is Holy. You are created as a free will spirit to love and serve God. Sin separates you from a holy God. Death is the judicial price required to pay for your sins and it is on the head of every sinner. Jesus came to be the Lamb of God, God's sacrifice, to pay the price for your sins by the sacrifice of himself. Christ proved he was from God by being raised from the dead and appearing to many witnesses. When you understand and believe this and are willing to confess Christ's name and repent of your sins, you can be baptized *into* Christ and into His death. You are thus united with His death, your sins are removed, and your spiritual relationship with a holy God is restored. He then adds you to His kingdom, His church. In His kingdom you accept the headship of Christ and commit to a life of loving faithfulness to Christ's authority and commands as delivered by

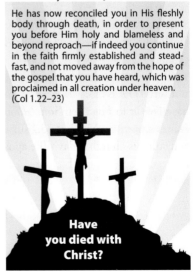

He has now reconciled you in His fleshly body through death, in order to present you before Him holy and blameless and beyond reproach—if indeed you continue in the faith firmly established and steadfast, and not moved away from the hope of the gospel that you have heard, which was proclaimed in all creation under heaven. (Col 1.22–23)

Have you died with Christ?

His apostles once for all. Jesus will return one day and then you will be judged according to your actions in this life. If found faithful, you will join with God in heaven, an eternal life of glory.

Once you are in Christ you can have great confidence of your salvation. Those that are committed to Christ have this promise: *"Be faithful until death, and I will give you the crown of life"* (Rev 2.10). If you further sin as a Christian, you can repent and ask God's forgiveness (1 John 2.1).

Jesus came to provide you with an abundant life (John 10.10). Not a life filled with an abundance of things, but a life filled with an abundance of hope. An abundance of hope based on the truth of the gospel and strength of faith in the promises of God (Col 1.23). An abundance of joy and fulfillment that can be found only in living a life of purpose focused on eternal life with a holy God (Matt 6.33).

The Old Testament taught us about God's grace and mercy, demonstrated by animal sacrifice paying the judicial price for sin. Against the Old Testament revelation is set God's Son, Jesus Christ, who is the climax of the drama, since through him God's work and revelation was brought to perfection.

This message is unique to Christianity. No other system, ideology, or religion proclaims a free forgiveness and a new life to those who have done nothing to deserve it but everything to deserve condemnation instead. On the contrary, all other systems teach some form of self-salvation through good works of religion, superstition, or self-enlightenment. The Bible, by contrast, teaches a gospel, *the* gospel, good news that God's grace has turned away His deserved wrath, that His Son has paid our price of death, that God has shown mercy on the undeserving. We have, and cannot contribute anything to His grace. Faith's function is to accept the free gift that God's grace offers and live our lives accordingly.

Gospels of every hue and description darken the landscape like a cloud of hungry locusts that indiscriminately devour everything in their path. Yet a single ray of objective truth pierces through the darkness offering hope to all who embrace it. This gospel reflects the unity and time tested truth of the Bible. This gospel and this gospel alone will accomplish all that the Creator has purposed for His creation. It is a beacon of hope offered by a loving Father to His children—a light that bathes the cross of the Lamb of God.

Receiving the Gift

Confess your belief, Matthew 10.32–33; **Repent** of your sins, Acts 2.38, 2 Peter 3.9; Be **Baptized** for the remission of your sins, Acts 2.38; **Live Faithfully** until death, Revelation 2.10, 2 Peter 3.17

Buy in Bulk and Save

Want to buy multiple copies of this book for your friends, family, or congregation? Buy in bulk and save:

Quantity	Cost
1–4	$6.99
5–9	$5.99
10–24	$4.99
25–99	$3.99
100+	$2.99

Church pricing special: Sealed Case for $299 (128 books at $2.34 per book)

To place an order, please contact:

DeWard Publishing Company, Ltd.
P.O. Box 6259
Chillicothe, Ohio 45601
www.dewardpublishing.com

800.300.9778
dan@dewardpublishing.com

Shipping charges will be added. Wholesale orders (40% discount) require minimum purchase of 100 books. Large orders may require additional time, depending on inventory. Please allow at least two weeks for orders of 1,000 or more.

For a full listing of DeWard Publishing Company books, visit our website:

www.deward.com